T0095004

There is a Balm for That

REGINA R. TATE

ILLUSTRATIONS BY BRAELON M. TATE

authorHOUSE®

AuthorHouse™ LLC
1663 Liberty Drive
Bloomington, IN 47403
www.authorhouse.com
Phone: 1-800-839-8640

© 2014 Regina R. Tate. All rights reserved.

No part of this book may be reproduced, stored in a retrieval system, or
transmitted by any means without the written permission of the author.

Published by AuthorHouse 05/21/2014

ISBN: 978-1-4969-1484-2 (sc)
ISBN: 978-1-4969-1485-9 (e)

Scripture quotations marked NIV are taken from the Holy Bible, New International
Version®. NIV®. Copyright © 1973, 1978, 1984 by International Bible Society.
Used by permission of Zondervan. All rights reserved. [Biblica]

Any people depicted in stock imagery provided by Thinkstock are models,
and such images are being used for illustrative purposes only.
Certain stock imagery © Thinkstock.

This book is printed on acid-free paper.

Because of the dynamic nature of the Internet, any web addresses or links contained in
this book may have changed since publication and may no longer be valid. The views
expressed in this work are solely those of the author and do not necessarily reflect the
views of the publisher, and the publisher hereby disclaims any responsibility for them.

Contents

Preface

History records that on January 14, 2003, the Kentucky Wildcat men's basketball team started a most unlikely winning streak. Before the season began, one contributing player was dismissed from the team and two more major contributors to the team were suspended, upsetting chemistry and leaving the team short-handed. The season was the 100th one in the history of the program and it was not turning out as the imagined celebratory season everyone had hoped for. The previous year's team had been dubbed Team Turmoil and this squad was showing a great many similarities.

Sometimes we find ourselves in a state such as this. Bad stuff keeps piling up on us and before we can solve one crisis, another one comes, or we are blindsided by an event or occurrence that is draining all our energy and we are weary. Or we, and those around us, are down on ourselves because it seems our lot presents a continuous, negative pattern. Or perhaps we should be celebrating a milestone as we planned and nothing is going according to plan. This collection of writings is for all of us at just such times. From this volume we can find encouragement to get us over or get us through. In it, we are reminded that we are never alone and at any time, we can begin our own winning streak. (For more on that Kentucky basketball team, see Building the Kingdom.)

The world presents so much (pain, chaos, temptation, illicitness, immorality, sinful pleasures, etc . . . .) and sometimes we Christians find ourselves too close to the edge of the Vineyard (read The Vineyard to see what I mean). I use real-world examples coupled with God's Word to direct people back to God. The truth is all the direction and guidance we need is in there—in the Bible. Most of the relatable stories have to do with sports (a true love of mine) but there is no need to worry if you are not a sports fan. The references enhance the primary messages of inspiration; the main thing is still the main thing. (I'm laughing to myself now because I say that and then move to . . . .)

In his acceptance speech, for the National Basketball Association's 2014 Most Valuable Player award, Kevin Durant spoke of God changing his life and how basketball was just a platform for him to inspire people. (He wasn't the first Christian athlete to voice recognition of purpose but perhaps the most passionate.) He spoke of wanting to be a recreation league coach. While he would have still been in an arena that allowed him to inspire people, how awesome is it that God guided him into increased territory (using his mom to push him into it)? His childhood was not easy. He experienced a great deal of uncertainty and went through many trials before his winning streak began (and the streak pertains to more than just basketball).

Sometimes our troubles come because we get caught up with our plans, our goals or our expectations and we end up fighting against the very blessing we have petitioned God for. We effectively delay some of the blessings God is willing to bestow upon us because we won't move out of the way. At other times, we squirm away from our path because we don't recognize our preparation as of God. I believe this particular platform is mine, to help us learn to let go and let God "mold us and make us after His will, while we are waiting, yielded and still (Have Thine Own Way Lord by Adelaide Pollard)."

The book primarily speaks to Christians or those leaning toward Christ but it also holds messages for all of God's children, be they acknowledging or not. And just so you know, all of the scriptural references are from the New International Version, unless otherwise noted. My prayer is that you dig deeper and renew your strength by getting back to the source of life; the creator of heaven and earth. Let Him lead and guide you as you rest comfortably in His arms (see explanation of the paradox throughout the book and specifically in Gifts of the Cross).

Regina

Building the Kingdom

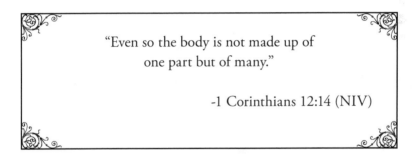

"Even so the body is not made up of
one part but of many."

-1 Corinthians 12:14 (NIV)

Original Post—May 23, 2013

Building the Kingdom

I recently watched an animated movie with the family and discovered, once again, that the movie had a thinly-veiled biblical theme. The basic premise of most of these movies is the same; good triumphs over evil, love over hate. There are varying levels of adversity that must be overcome during the conflicts but they are always overcome. The protagonist builds necessary character and learns to be a team player in order to fulfill his or her destiny and save the day, with or without assistance. There is much reward for the change of heart and there are a plethora of benefits that accompany the personal growth. It never gets old. The Bible is such a great model for everything.

I love team sports and at the moment, I am enthralled with the journey to the 2013 NBA finals. The Miami Heat team is my team and I am pulling hard for them. But I chuckled to myself the other day when I had the occasion to read a paper I wrote for a class some years ago. The paper included references to the 2002-2003 Kentucky Wildcats male basketball team.

The 2002-2003 basketball season was the fifth of Orlando "Tubby" Smith's coaching tenure at Kentucky and the program was celebrating 100 years in existence. The storied basketball program was to be on display for the celebration. However, for a while, it didn't look as if they would make it to the party. Jason Parker had been dismissed, Erik Daniels had been suspended for four games and Cliff Hawkins, the starting point guard, was academically ineligible for the coinciding first semester of play. Then, at the start of the season, Antwain Barbour broke his hand. The season before, the team had been dubbed Team Turmoil and this team was stacking up to look very similar to that one. On December 28, 2002, the team suffered its third loss and the Lexington faithful were starting to think this year of celebration was turning into another season of reproach.

In theory, on the division one college level, everybody who suits up for the team is capable of contributing to the team's success, in one way or another.

Tubby knew this and just needed his team to believe while he found ways to maximize what he was working with. History would record that this roster had no first or second team All-Americans on it. But a coach who believes, and can get his players to buy in, can do marvelous things.

In the absence of Daniels, Hawkins and Barbour, Keith Bogans stepped into a leadership role and Gerald Fitch was filling in wherever he was asked—playing more than the point guard position. Chuck Hayes was blossoming in his sophomore season and Marquis Estill and Jules Camara were holding it down inside. By the beginning of January, Tubby had gotten back his injured and suspended players (his crucial depth) and he rolled them into the team without public drama or problems with chemistry.

And then, on January 14, 2003, the eleven win—three loss Kentucky Wildcats were in Nashville to battle the Vanderbilt Commodores. The first quarter was in the books with Vanderbilt in firm control and the second quarter seemed to be heading down the drain for the Wildcats. Then, the proverbial light seemed to go on for the Wildcats as coach Tubby appeared to be losing his mind. The Commodores took a 36-28 lead into halftime but went home with a 74-52 loss to mull over.

It was a magnificent display of defensive intensity and offensive efficiency by Kentucky. It was the glorious start of the 26-game winning-steak. (The streak was halted during the Elite Eight game of the NCAA tournament that featured an injury-weakened Kentucky Wildcat team against the Dwyane Wade-led Marquette Golden Eagles.) The Wildcats were successful because Tubby was able to pull potential out of all of his players so that he could put together game plans that capitalized on their strengths; he put them in positions to be successful. It was awesome to watch.

Eric Spoelstra's task has always been the same but different. I love watching the Heat play. Their defensive intensity and efficient offense are remarkable because of the *big three*. There are some who discount the coaching job Spoelstra has done because his roster includes LeBron James, Dwyane Wade and Chris Bosh. Let me say that there have been many rosters that boasted All-American and All-World type players and those units were unable to reach the pinnacles of their professions because they did not operate as efficient and effective teams. It's a tough sell for coaches whose players have been superior individual talents all of their lives. They are asked to dim the light to dim the light a bit and find ways to help their team be successful. For me, that makes the job that Eric Spoelstra has done all the more remarkable. He has gotten his players to trust; to trust him and to trust each other.

That's how it works in the body of Christ. Everybody's strengths are different and while you may be dominant and your light may shine brighter, mine still shines for someone to see. God is able to maximize my gifts while at the same time illuminating yours. We just need to trust Him. In 1 Corinthians 12:14, 18-20, the ideal coalescence of and the function of the body of Christ—the team so to speak—is outlined; "the body is not made up of one part but of many . . . . But in fact God has placed the parts in the body, every one of them, just as He wanted them to be. If they were all one part, where would the body be? As it is, there are many parts, but one body."

We all have a part to play, a contribution to make to the team. Your tasks may be similar to mine but they are not the same. We just have to trust that God knows what he's doing in preparing us and positioning us. He wants us all to be successful so He will put us in positions to win and perhaps start our own winning streaks.

If we would stop fixating on and coveting the positions of others, we could concentrate on the development of our talents and our gifts. We could strengthen our position, thereby strengthening the Body. If all of us would do that, our team would be awesome.

Regina

Probing Deeper:

What are my initial thoughts?

What did I learn or reinforce while reading this?

Can what I learned or reinforced help me with my daily life? If so, how?

Am I experiencing something right now that this particular inspiration can help me with?

Can I lighten the load someone else is experiencing by sharing this inspiration? If so, who is it and how will I do it?

Comfort in Knowing

"Then the end will come, when He hands over the kingdom to God the Father after He has destroyed all dominion, authority and power."

-1 Corinthians 15:24 (NIV)

Original Post—June 13, 2013

Comfort in Knowing

It always fascinates me when people tell me they have recorded a sporting event, or any other continuing saga, and expect that they will not hear the results prior to watching the recording. Given the communal times in which we live, it's laughable to believe that the results won't find you in some way. I don't have that problem with results though. I can know the end and still enjoy the journey, or at least benefit from it in some way. Knowing the end does alleviate a certain level of stress but, I still experience all of the highs and lows and I enjoy the intensity just the same—or at least I believe I do. I recently went to see the latest requisite movie for all supporters of the United Federation of Planets. The movie was extremely intense and (though reality was suspended quite a few times during the duration) I absolutely loved it.

These prequels are remarkable in that the writers and producers are able to tell a story, build interest and have people sit on the edge of their seats, all the while knowing that the major players survive whatever the trials are because we know them in a future timeline. During the movie I saw, I had to keep reminding myself that all of them survive; Kirk would make it with Spock, Uhuru (in all of her newly infused prominence), Sulu, Bones, Scotty and Chekov in tow. I had to keep breathing as the epic battle, with a familiar enemy, was set up for the battle that has already taken place. The movie was awesome and I was quickly reminded of another epic story whose end I know. The story, with all of its ending glory, was written many, many centuries ago.

When we become Christians and embrace the inerrant Word of God, we learn the truth; the truth about the ending as we begin our journey toward it. How great is that? We learn that Christ is victorious; He has already conquered death and the grave. And we, who have accepted Him as our Lord and Savior, are victorious and have been reconciled to God because of Christ's atonement for our sins. We know the end, even as our trials and tribulations lead to doubt of our personal victory. We know the end, even as the evil-one seeks to make us believe he has the final say. We know the end, even as terrible things continue to happen all around us and sometimes to us. We know the end, even as our personal struggles seem to knock the life out of us. We know the end, even as God must break us from habits that do not serve His purposes or ours.

He told us that He works in the midst of all things so that, together, all things work for our good and for His purposes (Romans 8:28). If we take God at His word (and all Christians should), we know that even though we walk through what may seem like the valley with a shadow that seems like death, we should really fear no evil because He is always with us, strengthening us for our particular journey (Psalms 23). We know that even if this mortal life ends, it is not the END. We have a home not made by hand but, a home that is eternal in the heavens (2 Corinthians 5:1). We have a home where the wicked will cease from troubling us and the weary ones of us will be at rest (Job 3:17). Oh what Good News! It's too good to keep to ourselves. Shouldn't the knowing make us bolder witnesses, more assured in our walks of faith? Upon introspection, is there more we should be doing to spread the News?

Regina

Probing Deeper:

What are my initial thoughts?

What did I learn or reinforce while reading this?

Can what I learned or reinforced help me with my daily life? If so, how?

Am I experiencing something right now that this particular inspiration can help me with?

Can I lighten the load someone else is experiencing by sharing this inspiration? If so, who is it and how will I do it?

Knowing More

"I pray that out of his glorious riches he may strengthen you with power through his Spirit in your inner being, so that Christ may dwell in your hearts through faith."

-Ephesians 3:16-17a (NIV)

Original Post—June 27, 2013

Knowing More

So how much is too much? I was thinking about that as I watched the two basketball teams representing their respective conferences before the seventh game of the 2013 NBA finals. I always marvel at the lather of sweat these athletes work up before a game. Game six of the series had pushed the players beyond normal limits of emotion and exhaustion. Now, the San Antonio Spurs and the Miami Heat were preparing for what was a fantabulous game seven. So really, how much of a warm up is enough? How much energy do you expend before the actual competition begins in order to get your body ready to perform, while making sure you have the energy required to play, and hopefully, win the game? The answer is, of course, that these elite athletes started unique relationships with their bodies long before we ever heard their names. They pushed and cajoled and pushed and demanded and pushed and rested and pushed and pleaded until they could hear their bodies talking to them; feel their bodies' need for one thing or another.

In game five of the 1997 NBA finals, the game that has come to be known as the flu game, the Chicago Bulls and the Utah Jazz had each won two games. The site of game five was Utah and the day before the game, Michael Jordan had flu-like symptoms as a result of a stomach virus or some sort of food poisoning. Whatever the case, Jordan was visibly pale and noticeably weak. His trainer told him that there was no way he would be able to play in game five. Oh but Michael had put the work in! He knew what his body could do because he had been there and pushed it for years. He had a relationship and an understanding of his body that no one else had—not even his trainer.

So what of the rest of us? How many of us push the way athletes do? After giving our lives to Christ, do we learn of Him, testing the limits of our Alliance? Are we familiar with the advantages of close and intimate relationship with Him? After years of practice and competition, athletes have a pretty firm grip on their capabilities; on what is necessary to nurture and nourish their bodies in order to perform. In the Alliance with Christ, are we cultivating and nurturing the relationship for optimum performance? (We need to be doing similar things in marriage, with the three-stranded cord, but that's a story for another day).

If properly cultivated, our Alliance will allow us to run headlong into our fears; to run through a fire wearing the gasoline drawers we sometimes feel we have on. We are assured that when we encounter deep waters, we won't drown and when we walk through fire, we won't burn because God is with us (Isaiah 43:2-3). And we have an added bonus; we have a Spirit that lives within, guiding us and bringing things to our remembrance (John 14:26). What excuse do we have for not maximizing our personal Alliance? If we are diligent about our learning and if we exercise our knowledge, we can really experience increasing snatches of heaven right here on earth. Our fluid goal, as Christians, is to look more and more like Christ, to act more and more like Him. Are we moving in the direction of the goal; getting to know Him more completely; understanding what we can expect from Him; maximizing the benefits of the Alliance?

Regina

Probing Deeper:

What are my initial thoughts?

What did I learn or reinforce while reading this?

Can what I learned or reinforced help me with my daily life? If so, how?

Am I experiencing something right now that this particular inspiration can help me with?

Can I lighten the load someone else is experiencing by sharing this inspiration? If so, who is it and how will I do it?

Hold Fast

"I consider that our present sufferings are not worth comparing with the glory that will be revealed in us."

-Romans 8:18 (NIV)

Original Post—July 18, 2013

Hold Fast

Years ago I heard a song by James Bignon and the Deliverance Mass Choir that stuck with me. Part of the refrain says "hold fast, hold fast, your troubles will not last. There's a blessing on the other side of through." Whenever the Holy Spirit brings that song to my remembrance, I feel empowered to hold on for as long as God says I can. Going through can seem ominous, making us look for shortcuts or detours but, the shortest distance between two points is a straight line. So even if we have to dig our own tunnel to get to the other side, we may as well get to it.

The funny thing is we often pray to God for more, forgetting that more will challenge us. And God really wants us to have what we ask for so He allows our testing to come to make us better, to make us ready. Our trials may often be torturous and the accompanying pain may be excruciating but our job is to learn and to bring glory to God while acknowledging that we will only understand in part, trusting in the one who loves us unconditionally, the one who is omnipotent and omniscient, the one who can see the entire picture.

Our current living space is so perverted. Principles and priorities are misaligned, values are misplaced, truth has levels, degrees and perspectives while biases paralyze, maim and kill. It is assured that we will be misunderstood for doing the right thing; we will be mocked for our beliefs. But God cares about our character, not necessarily our reputation; He is building us to last. We may lose much and many but, if we remain steadfast, He will successfully transform our minds for increased understanding—partial but increasing—as long as we do "what's right, love mercy and walk humbly with our God (Micah 6:8)."

Brian Banks is fighting to make the 53-man roster of the Atlanta Falcons this season. Many folks with no affection for football and some casual fans of the game will join in with rabid fans of the Falcons in pulling for Brian to make the team. Brian's testimony has endeared him to many of us. Eleven years ago, Brian was on his way to the University of Southern

California, on a full scholarship, to study and play out his passion on the gridiron. Instead, Brian spent almost 11 years away from the game and the pursuit of his dream—to play professional football. On Brian's 18th birthday, he went to prison for a rape that never happened. His accuser lied because he made her angry (sounds like Potiphar's wife). The lie was inconsistent and there was no concrete evidence, still Brian went to jail. Unfortunately, Brian's attorney was unwilling to stare down stereotypes in order to defend her client.

Brian says he felt pressured to accept a plea deal without the presence or counsel of his mother. He acquiesced to his attorney's wishes rather than standing on the truth, the truth that God rejoices in. Stripped down, isn't that the choice we consistently have to make? Still, God will cause all things to work together for our good if we love Him and are about his business (Romans 8:28).

We won't all suffer the way Brian did but we will all come to a place where we will have to run through, walk through or are pushed through. As a result, we will learn more about ourselves and more about God and the grace and mercy that can see us through. Brian isn't bitter and he has been blessed mightily since coming out on the other side of through and it isn't over yet. The glorious news is God will work with him—and all of us—until the day of Christ Jesus (Philippians 1:6).

There are a myriad of blessings that come to us on the other side of through, not the least of which are perspective, humility and endurance, all of which make Brian valuable to any NFL team (in my opinion) and will get us all closer to the image God sees when He looks at us through the lens of Jesus Christ. We become more effective and compassionate witnesses for the Lord. And just as there are a multitude of blessings that can come to us on the other side, there are many reasons for our journeys through the valleys that look like death. Whatever the reasons, everybody won't get it and some may fall off but, "if we endure, we will also reign with Him (2 Timothy 2:12)". We may have to encourage ourselves and that's fine as long as we hold fast, knowing our troubles will not last and there are blessings on the other side of through.

Regina

Probing Deeper:

What are my initial thoughts?

What did I learn or reinforce while reading this?

Can what I learned or reinforced help me with my daily life? If so, how?

Am I experiencing something right now that this particular inspiration can help me with?

Can I lighten the load someone else is experiencing by sharing this inspiration? If so, who is it and how will I do it?

Being You

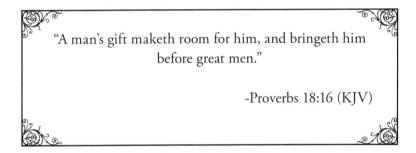

"A man's gift maketh room for him, and bringeth him
before great men."

-Proverbs 18:16 (KJV)

Original Post—August 8, 2013

Being You

The year 2013 marks the 25th Anniversary of the Heisman trophy season of one of the greatest running backs to ever play the game of football. Oklahoma State University (OSU) will celebrate the historic exploits of Barry Sanders. Excuse me, College Football and National League Football (NFL) Hall of Famer Barry Sanders. Sanders started at running back just one season at OSU, but in that one season he assaulted the Big Eight and NCAA record books. Not bad for someone who, in high school, had his starting tailback position wrested away from him by one of his brothers. Thank God he moved to running back!

At 5'8", Sanders wasn't heavily recruited. He ended up at OSU, playing behind future NFL Hall of Famer Thurman Thomas for two years. Sanders' one prodigious season was all he needed to prove he could play among the men already suiting up in the NFL. He vaulted to the NFL after that season, to the Detroit Lions. The Lions selected him third overall in the 1989 draft. He immediately commenced to writing his name all over the NFL annals. Then in July of 1999, after ten seasons with the Lions, he shocked the world and knocked his team off-balance when he announced his retirement, via fax. (Talk about going out on top!) After much speculation and consternation, Sanders finally admitted that the losing had started to affect his spirit and he was willing to let it go before it changed who he was.

In 2009, a certain married hedge fund analyst quit his job. This analyst held a BS in mathematics, a BS in electrical engineering and computer science, as well as an MS in computer science from the Massachusetts Institute of Technology and he held an MBA from the Harvard Business School (whew!). Five years earlier, Salman Khan's seventh grade cousin was struggling with math so he agreed to tutor her—remotely. He lived in Boston and she lived in his hometown of New Orleans so he would upload his tutorial sessions to YouTube. It turned out that his cousin wasn't the only one who benefited from the lessons.

People started making requests for lessons which led him to create a YouTube account so that he could regularly upload sessions. Finally he decided to quit his job and focus on what had become the Khan Academy: a non-profit learning institution initially run from a desk in one of Khan's closets. The mission of the non-profit is "to provide a free, world-class education for anyone, anywhere." His lessons caught the attention of Bill Gates. Gates found and used the lessons to teach his own kids. After his discovery, he set up a meeting with Khan and the rest is unfolding history. Sal Khan now has financial backing and is slowly changing the face of education. He and his very innovative team have been able to write software that measures the change they seek to make.

These two accounts represent myriads of others. The subjects followed the leading of the Lord or, as a lot of them would say, followed their hearts. It's so easy to get caught up, making mountains of money or having power or prestige or exercising privilege, that we can forget our original intentions. Or we may find our cause while following a path that was preparing us for the task God always had for us. Whichever the case, sometimes we have to leave our good job or our comfortable relationships to do what is true for us (and everybody won't understand). God may have us where we are to grow our character, while changing the culture and environment around us, or He may make it very plain that we are out-of-place. (Prayer and time with God is essential here.)

In our overarching mission to glorify God and draw others to Christ, we may have to hold fast (see Hold Fast), step out, step up or step over, and it will all be good as long as our steps are ordered by the Lord. We just have to remember that mistakes are darn near mandatory but patterns are detrimental and hiding-out is not acceptable. If we all get busy, we can change our living space for the better. Now go do your God-directed thing while I try to do mine!

Regina

Probing Deeper:

What are my initial thoughts?

What did I learn or reinforce while reading this?

Can what I learned or reinforced help me with my daily life? If so, how?

Am I experiencing something right now that this particular inspiration can help me with?

Can I lighten the load someone else is experiencing by sharing this inspiration? If so, who is it and how will I do it?

The Edge

> "I will put my laws in their minds and write them on their hearts. I will be their God, and they will be My people. No longer will they teach their neighbor, or say to one another, 'Know the Lord,' because they will all know Me, from the least of them to the greatest."
>
> -Hebrews 8:10b-11 (NIV)

Initial Appearance

The Edge

A few years ago, during Sunday School class, the conversation turned to our collective children. One of the gentlemen in the class was concerned that his children were growing up with advantages and privileges he couldn't even fathom during his childhood. As a result, his children had not and seemingly would not develop the edge he had developed growing up. He felt they would need the edge in order to survive. I smiled to myself because I once had a conversation with my dad that revealed he once had the same concerns.

My dad's childhood was challenging, to say the least. He grew up in Jackson, Mississippi, during the 1940s and 50s. And while he wished he could infuse us with his earned wisdom, he realized all he could do was recount stories for us and share the lessons he'd learned from each incident in hopes of curtailing our periods of pain and anguish (because he never let us believe that they would not come). He accepted that his experiences were his and that history and progress would never permit us to experience the environment nor the conditions that helped create the man he had become.

His job was to put it out there for us, desiring that we would benefit from the lessons he had shared. It's ironic that each generation grows up hoping to ease the burden of the one to follow and as we are able, we worry that we are somehow depriving our children by providing and protecting them. We want better for them even when we don't know what better looks like. I told the guy in the class not to worry about it, that God would have his children's backs. With God, we will always develop the edge we need.

A lot of today's truly gifted young athletes are spoiled and coddled. Athletic prowess and years of domination, coupled with all the adulation and praise, have borne in them senses of entitlement; entitled to always win, entitled to fairness, entitled to health and longevity in the sport just to name a few. They become accustomed to winning because they are able to accomplish so much—consistently. They develop and conquer intermediate and transitory *edges* every time they encounter new and greater competition. They push themselves to meet and beat every level of that competition on their way to the pinnacle of their sport. So when clouds of adversity show up (in the form of losing streaks, personal slumps, absent praise), they find themselves in unchartered territory.

Many of these gifted athletes never had the occasion to develop the edge they will now need to protect their mind and spirit from what is happening outside of them. But if they have heard the word of the Lord from anybody along the way—God-fearing parents, a praying grandmother, from saved advisors, from Christian teammates—then it is likely that they will find their way to the other side of through. On the other side, they will have developed the *edge* they need to step up on in order to view things from a higher perspective. And from the ledge that was once the edge, they will learn that what they do is merely a platform to do what God has really intended for them to do (thanks again Kevin Durant).

In Paul's first letter to the believers at Corinth, he deals with a few issues. The first has to do with what he has heard about the fighting and the divisions happening among them. The people are dividing themselves into camps based on the leadership. Paul is taken aback. He reminds them that he nor Apollos nor any of the other leaders died for them. They were all just flesh and blood, seeking to lead all of them to Christ who was crucified for them.

"What, after all, is Apollos? And what is Paul? Only servants, through whom you came to believe—as the Lord has assigned to each his task. I planted the seed, Apollos watered it, but God has been making it grow. So neither the one who plants nor the one who waters is anything, but only God, who makes things grow . . . . For we are co-workers in God's service; you are God's field, God's building. By the grace God has given me, I laid a foundation as a wise builder, and someone else is building on it. But each one should build with care. For no one can lay any foundation other than the one already laid, which is Jesus Christ (1 Corinthians 3:5-11)."

As parents, it's not our job to save our children. We don't need to deprive them of anything we are able to provide in hopes that they will develop an *edge* and neither do we need to shelter them from the world around them in an effort to protect them. They will learn what they need to know one way or another. As parents or coaches or advisors or people of influence, we just need to handle our tasks, making sure we are planting the right types of seeds and spreading adequate water; building our children atop the foundation that is Christ. If we do that, God will provide the increase. God has all of our backs!

Regina

Probing Deeper:

What are my initial thoughts?

What did I learn or reinforce while reading this?

Can what I learned or reinforced help me with my daily life? If so, how?

Am I experiencing something right now that this particular inspiration can help me with?

Can I lighten the load someone else is experiencing by sharing this inspiration? If so, who is it and how will I do it?

There's a Balm for That

"Even though I walk through the darkest valley, I will fear no evil, for You are with me; Your rod and Your staff, they comfort me."

-Psalms 23:4 (NIV)

Original Post—August 30, 2013

There's a Balm for That

This is the most wonderful time of the year; fall is in the air and football is on the ground. The youth football season started last week, college football started this past Thursday night and I am anxiously awaiting the beginning of the real NFL season. My joy abounds. Still, there are days when I hurt all over.

My head hurts because there is so little tolerance for the diverse prisms through which we see life and there is a declining appreciation for the myriad ways we have come to survive life. My neck hurts because I snap it every time somebody fails to understand that you can't continuously cripple a class of people and then demand that they govern themselves like those of privilege. My eyes hurt from having to witness the blatant lack of compassion and the many injustices that plague our world. My ears hurt from having to listen to people lie—even when they know the truth—just so they can hold on to power. My stomach hurts because I sometimes swallow my words when I want to admonish those who are influencing children in a generational-curse-kind of way. My feet hurt from just trying to keep up amid tight schedules and accumulating birthdays. My heart hurts because we were (and are) all born into sin and, the awful fact is, too many of us will continue to wallow there, without the feeling of love, without the guidance of God. But this is not a woe is me diatribe. I have medicine; I have a Balm in Gilead!

All of us were created in the image and likeness of God—all of us. But we were (are) born into sin with a connection that is dormant, inoperative. God can't look upon sin, so He gave us another way to get to Him; He sent His Son to save us—to atone for us. So whenever God looks at us, He is looking through the blood of Jesus (Romans 5:9). In essence, we were born heading straight into eternal darkness, destruction and despair—going to hell in a hand-basket. But somewhere, on our personal Damascus Road, we had an encounter with Christ that saved our lives.

During the encounter, we chose to believe the Good News and when we believed, we were justified and our profession of faith saved us (Romans

10:10). Our connection to God changed our trajectory; we began moving on up! Our x-axis continued to move horizontally while our y-axis began its vertical assent. (This is why good without God is wonderful in order to get along with people and to avoid earthly consequences, but it will do nothing for you eternally.) We are now functioning branches attached to The Awesome Vine (John 15:5); capable of doing anything because Christ strengthens us (Philippians 4:13).

Peyton and Eli Manning had an NFL quarterback for a dad and were predisposed to play that position in the NFL. The Matthews family business is professional football. Doc River's son Austin grew up with basketball and now plays in the NBA. John H. Johnson created a brand that his daughter, Linda Johnson Rice, now oversees. And the list goes on that way. But we tell children that they can be anything they set their minds to be. And while that is true, it is hard to accomplish a shift alone.

The key is God Himself, who is able to do abundantly above anything we can think or ask Him to do (Ephesians 3:20). Arthur Ashe covered unchartered territory, playing championship tennis. Gabby Douglas stepped out on faith, going away from the family, and won Olympic gold—twice. President Barack Obama's dad—well you know the story. And the list goes on that way. Somewhere along their journeys, there was a deliberate changing in the path that started the assent upward, even in a metaphorical foreign land.

There are too many stories of people giving up and giving in. As was said in a previous blog; "in our mission to glorify God and draw others to Christ, we may have to hold fast, step out, step up or step over." Whatever it takes, we need to get the word out and get the human display on. Everybody needs to know that "there is a balm in Gilead, to make the wounded whole; there is a balm in Gilead to heal the sin-sick soul . . . If you cannot sing like angels, if you can't preach like Paul, you can tell of the love of Jesus and say He died for all (Negro Spiritual of unknown origin)." Be blessed!

Regina

Probing Deeper:

What are my initial thoughts?

What did I learn or reinforce while reading this?

Can what I learned or reinforced help me with my daily life? If so, how?

Am I experiencing something right now that this particular inspiration can help me with?

Can I lighten the load someone else is experiencing by sharing this inspiration? If so, who is it and how will I do it?

Called to Be Better

"But you are a chosen people, a royal priesthood, a holy nation, God's special possession, that you may declare the praises of Him who called you out of darkness into His wonderful light."

-1 Peter 2:9 (NIV)

Original Post—October 15, 2013

Called to Be Better

I've been thinking a lot lately about homogeneity and the groupthink that is often a by-product of it. All of it makes me hurt (see blog six). Loosely homogeneous groups lack divergent perspectives and discriminable points of view. As a consequence, groupthink (defined as a pattern of thought characterized by self-deception, forced manufacture of consent, and conformity to group values and ethics) runs amok—rarely checked by group members of conscience. Lawmakers, who are to represent the best interests of the nation, stand in complicit agreement with liars and hate-mongers. A famed neurosurgeon, one once worthy of being called a role-model in my book, seems to have been sucked in as well. Groupthink is a mother . . . . -shut your mouth!

Groupthink is very dangerous. Because the rhetoric can feed upon itself, an alternate reality is often created. In the parallel universe, empathy, sympathy and civility are reserved for members only. Since members are the only ones who matter in their world, there is little or no remorse for the pain and anguish inflicted on folks outside of the group; the principle is paramount and everything and everybody else is expendable collateral. The original homogeneous members will use whatever and whoever they have to in order to reach their goals and then, the used up collateral is cast aside. Groupthink can cause fair-minded people to loose sensibilities and inhibitions. Forgotten is the notion that it is possible to be sane and dignified while in opposition. We can all fall prey. It's scary to believe but it can happen. We can sometimes find ourselves swept-up and acting crazy because we didn't stop to think; didn't stand for right but instead acquiesced to wrong.

Heading into the 2013-2014 football season, five players were dismissed from the Vanderbilt University football team; four of them were banned from campus. The fifth student, a former football captain, was banned from the football team. Chris Boyd was suspended from the team for attempting to cover-up a rape committed by four underclassmen. This is a heinous case of groupthink; an all too familiar one. While Chris Boyd may have had reservations about protecting his teammates, he ultimately decided to protect his brethren in the locker room. Chris Boyd was apparently not strong enough to step out of the box to finger the guilty young men and, begin the healing process for the victim. So rather than playing his senior season and solidifying his place in the NFL draft, he has possibly ruined his future. I know there is often a lot of gray area shaded around us at times but, we have to remember the question (from the very flawed questioner), "what would Jesus do?"

On an E:60 report, Arianna Clay recounted her assault by a senior officer within the U. S. Marine Corps. One night, she went to a gathering that made her very uncomfortable. She described the atmosphere as surprisingly fraternity-like so she decided to leave. As she was leaving, a drunken senior officer asked her to go fetch something. She said no and walked home. Four hours later, alone in her house, she was awakened. The officer had come to exact some revenge for her saying no to him—and he brought a civilian friend. Initially, the friend tried to get the officer to leave but in the end, he followed the officer in raping Arianna Clay. She reported the incident and was labeled a troublemaker before eventually being discharged. The sexual predator got a slap on the wrist for calling Mrs. Clay a slut during the attack. My mouth is still open.

Groupthink is insidious. The cultures (parallel universes) are not created overnight. Impressionable male athletes hear girls downgraded constantly on their fields and courts of play (you run like a girl, you hit like a girl, stop whining like a girl) and the unstable ones among them look to exact control and power over something or someone. Guess who they choose. In the armed forces, as a consequence of history, the decision-making commanding officers look just alike (my own observation as they testified before Congress). Back when these men were recruits, there were probably attitudes regarding women that would make our skin crawl. The culture was formed around those attitudes and the core thoughts and beliefs of that culture apparently remain.

The officers are fighting for the right to maintain the disgusting and inexcusable system that continually blames the victim in cases of sexual assault—they are fighting to maintain their power. While there may be some officers within the ranks who believe that the decisions regarding a case's merit should be determined objectively, groupthink keeps them virtually silent. In the meantime, hundreds continue to be assaulted by the predators within the ranks of brave men and women who take seriously their commitment to protect and serve.

God is calling us to greater than just walking in lock-step. He wants us to build meaningful relationships among people; we are to spread His love, grace and mercy among all people. When He gives us opportunities to further His message, we should take them—step out of the box and take them. The youngest among us are often the catalysts for change because their experiences don't yet limit their optimism or their conquering spirit.

Malala Yousafzai is an advocate for the education of girls in her native Pakistan. A risky proposition for sure but her family encourages her to do what she believes in. One day, during Malala's twelfth year of existence, a member of the Taliban shot her three times at point blank range. Malala miraculously survived because God orchestrated it that way. She is now more resolute in her fight for educational equality and her audience of supporters has grown so much that she was nominated for the Nobel Peace Prize in 2013. While she didn't win the Nobel Award, she won the $65,000 Sakharov Award, Europe's top human rights award and her 16th birthday found her speaking before the assembly of the United Nations. What others meant for evil, God is still turning to good.

Bethany Hamilton lost an arm to a shark when she was thirteen. In the process of healing, she fortified her footing. One month after the attack, the Soul-Surfer returned to the water. One year later, she was back in championship form. Bethany Hamilton is an example of what happens when encouraging words and thoughtful prayer converge. Bethany and her family were always aligned with God's priorities, so moving beyond and moving on was not an option but a mandate. God has expanded Bethany's territory and her testimony continues to motivate millions to move beyond their particular calamity.

We all know stories of major overcoming and we are temporarily inspired to overcome ourselves. My challenge to all of us is to remain inspired by a God who changes not. We need to deepen our connection to God and to remain available to God. Groupthink is not a viable option and we cannot allow our distasteful experiences to limit our willingness to fight for what's right. Edmund Burke said long ago that "all that is required for evil to prevail is for good men to do nothing."

If the Lord calls us to "have seven priests carry trumpets of rams' horns in front of the ark. (And then) on the seventh day, march around the city seven times, with the priests blowing the trumpets. (Then) when you hear them sound a long blast on the trumpets, have the whole army give a loud shout; then the wall of the city will collapse and the army will go up, everyone straight in (Joshua 6:4-5)," we are to be obedient. If all looks bleak because an enemy that is seemingly more powerful than us is coming our way with fire in their eyes, we should seek the Lord's guidance.

Perhaps He will tell us: "Do not be afraid or discouraged because of this vast army. For the battle is not yours, but God's . . . . You will not have to fight this battle. Take up your positions; stand firm and see the deliverance the Lord will give you . . . . Do not be afraid; do not be discouraged. Go out to face them and the Lord will be with you (2 Chronicles 20:15-17)." We need to get busy and get beyond ourselves. If we are connected then we are assured that God will cause all things to work together for our good (Romans 8:28). We just have to keep pressing forward, to see what the end is going to be.

Regina

Probing Deeper:

What are my initial thoughts?

What did I learn or reinforce while reading this?

Can what I learned or reinforced help me with my daily life? If so, how?

Am I experiencing something right now that this particular inspiration can help me with?

Can I lighten the load someone else is experiencing by sharing this inspiration? If so, who is it and how will I do it?

The Favor of God

> "If you say, 'The Lord is my refuge,' and you make the Most High your dwelling, no harm will overtake you, no disaster will come near your tent."
>
> -Psalms 91:9-10 (NIV)

Original Post—September 19, 2013

The Favor of God

I recently read about Christian Ballard and I was shouting by the end of the article. Ballard played in the NFL for two years and recognized that he was becoming selfish and was developing an air of superiority. He left the Minnesota Vikings on August 18, 2013, and got married a couple of weeks later. Ballard, a Christian, acknowledged that there were many strong believers of Christ in the NFL and while they were able to maintain who they were at the core, he just couldn't pull it off. No doubt the transition away from football will be tough for him, at 24 years old, but I believe God will bless his efforts to be a good husband and a present and active father. Ballard doesn't rule out a return to the league (teams will always need defensive lineman with experience) but for now, he has recognized a need greater than money—a need for God and His priorities. (Fantasia told us that sometimes you have to lose to win again.)

Daniel and his friends, Hananiah, Mishael and Azariah (you may know them by the names given to them by the Babylonians; Belteshazzar, Shadrach, Meshach and Abednego) were Israelite royalty and were taken into captivity with their people by the Babylonians. The guys were identified as young men of royal descent who were without "any physical defect, handsome, showing aptitude for every kind of learning, well informed, quick to understand, and qualified to serve in the king's palace . . . . The king assigned them a daily amount of food and wine from the king's table. They were to be trained for three years, and after that they were to enter the king's service" (Daniel 1:4-5).

Well, you know how that went; Daniel struck a deal for them to eat according to their own beliefs and they entered the king's service healthier than their counterparts. "At the end of the time set by the king to bring them into his service, the chief official presented them to Nebuchadnezzar. The king talked with them, and he found none equal to Daniel, Hananiah, Mishael and Azariah . . . . In every matter of wisdom and understanding about which the king questioned them, he found them ten times better than all the magicians and enchanters in his whole kingdom. They were favored and Daniel became a trusted advisor" (Daniel 1:18-20). God used the tests and trials of the young men to open the eyes of others and to draw others to Himself. (Do the lion's den and the fiery furnace ring any bells?).

In the midst of prosperity, Christian Ballard had to let it go and, in the midst of captivity, Daniel and his friends found favor and were able to thrive. If we make steps toward God, we will be rewarded with His favor. He will take care of intermingling circumstances, intersecting paths and the timing that is so hard to master alone. Michael Dwayne Vick was written off by many after the stupidity that landed him in prison and away from football for two years. Vick's dog-fighting escapades and his arrogance left him broke and publicly shamed. But during that time, God dispatched some earthly angels to counsel with him and to help him map out his goals and regain his stability. After God got his attention, He was able to bless him.

Andy Reid was convinced that Vick had value and could help his Philadelphia Eagles team win. He felt that they could handle the circus that would surely come with Vick's signing, if the front office would just allow him to coach while they handled the other stuff (no easy trick after the whole Terrell Owens debacle). What Andy could not have known is that God was about to work some things out for the man who had come clean before Him and had clawed his way back into His presence.

In 2009, Vick signed a two-year contract with the Eagles. At the time, he was the third-team quarterback. By the end of that season, Reid had made the decision to move on from Donovan McNabb. Kevin Kolb was slated as the starter for the 2010 season; Vick his backup. One week into the season, Kolb suffered a concussion that allowed Vick to step back into a starting role and solidify his presence in Philly. God's favor is awesome and His grace is amazing! There are tremendous benefits for those who abide in His presence—no matter what (Job showed us that). Are you abiding—no matter what?

Regina

Probing Deeper:

What are my initial thoughts?

What did I learn or reinforce while reading this?

Can what I learned or reinforced help me with my daily life? If so, how?

Am I experiencing something right now that this particular inspiration can help me with?

Can I lighten the load someone else is experiencing by sharing this inspiration? If so, who is it and how will I do it?

The Vineyard

"Then they sat down and collected the good fish in baskets, but threw the bad away. This is how it will be at the end of the age. The angels will come and separate the wicked from the righteous and throw them into the blazing furnace, where there will be weeping and gnashing of teeth."

-Matthew 13:48b-50 (NIV)

Initial Appearance

The Vineyard

Jesus shares several parables that are outlined in the four Gospels (Matthew, Mark, Luke and John) in the New Testament. To the natural eye, the parables probably seem outrageous and foolish (I think He said they would), but thank God for the spiritual eye that allows us to see the lessons and the benefit that can be derived from all of them.

In Matthew 20, Jesus tells a parable about a landowner who hires many at different times of the day to come to work in his vineyard. With the first hired, he agrees to pay them a certain amount, for all of the others hired, he tells them he will pay them what is right. At the end of the day, the last hired (just an hour before quitting time) were paid first; they were paid what was promised to the first hired. The first hired stood, not-so-quietly, as all of the workers who came to work after them were paid a denarius.

When it came time for the 'firsts' to receive their pay, they protested the payment of one denarius because now they believed they deserved more. After all, they had worked all day in the heat, expending more energy and sweat than the others. The landowner was calm as he explained that they were being paid according to their agreement; he wasn't being unfair. As for the others hired, the landowner told them that it was his money to dispense with as he pleased. He could be kind and compassionate with his money if he wanted to be. And in verse 16, in the New Living Translation, Jesus is recorded as saying, "And so it is, that many who are first now will be last then; and those who are last now will be first then." The natural eye would have our view clouded and our vision blurred by personal desires and expectations. But, the spiritual eye would have us rejoicing because we are blessed in the field.

Perhaps many who are 'firsts' get discouraged or tired or weary in well doing. Instead of spending time working in the Vineyard to produce the path-altering fruit of the Spirit (that Paul lists for us in Galatians 5:22-33), perhaps 'firsts' are wasting time murmuring and complaining. Perhaps someone receives what was thought to be reserved for 'firsts' or others are getting what 'firsts thought they alone deserved. If not careful, 'firsts' can be drawn back toward the hiring line; drawn out of the Vineyard. Whatever the case, whatever the reason, if we wonder off and find ourselves in a place of darkness and isolation, close to the edge of the Vineyard, we need to stop moving and look up. And if we look up, we will become better simply by acknowledging and being in His presence—in His vineyard. And as we spend time adjusting our focus, we gain Godly perspective so that we can view situations differently.

We move back toward the communing of saints to find out we are not the first to go through this crisis and even now, we are not alone. We gladly attach ourselves to the new hires, showing them the ropes and expounding on the benefits of working in this Vineyard; teaching them how to work confidently through the storms and how to reposition themselves when they feel a struggle coming on. And we rejoice when others come into the Vineyard because we will be renewed by their energy, lifted by their praise. We are now effective workers for the Landowner; John calls us productive branches attached to the Vine in John 15:1-5. Either way, we are in His service, glorifying His name.

Braelon's christening was the public ceremony where we, his parents, acknowledged the covering of God and committed ourselves to being primary witnesses for Christ in the rearing of our son. We knew Braelon was covered until the age of consent, so we didn't pressure him to make any decisions regarding baptism. We just planted the seed and kept watering it. One Sunday, he told us that he had made the decision; he was going deeper with his own commitment. He had decided to publically declare what was already in his heart. Having made the decision, the onus is now on him to follow the teachings of Christ. We'll guide and teach him and we'll use every opportunity and life challenge to help him understand the need to dig deeper into his Holy relationship in order to go spiritually higher but praise God that he has taken his talents into the Vineyard himself.

As we walk, holding Braelon's hand, we know that we have a definite release date that will come with age. But praise God that our son has another hand. And he has joined his other hand to the man who stilled the water, the man who calmed the sea. As he walks and works in the Vineyard, he will continuously look at himself and in turn, see others differently because he put his hand in the hand of the Man from Galilee (Put Your Hand in the Hand by Ocean).

If you are one of the blessed ones entering the Vineyard after covering a long stretch of the world's highway, don't worry about your past and what others may bring up about you because of their own issues. (Katt Williams says the 'haters' are just doing their job—nothing personal.) None of us knew how to effectively work when we entered the Vineyard, no matter how some of us try to make it seem. Rest assured that if you confessed with your mouth and you believe in your heart, you are justified (for none of us are worthy) and safe in His Vineyard (Romans 10:9-10). So put your hand in the hand of the man from Galilee. Then run telling everybody you know to "come see a Man who told me everything I ever did (John 4:29)" and loves me still. Let all of the redeemed of the Lord say so!

Regina

Probing Deeper:

What are my initial thoughts?

What did I learn or reinforce while reading this?

Can what I learned or reinforced help me with my daily life? If so, how?

Am I experiencing something right now that this particular inspiration can help me with?

Can I lighten the load someone else is experiencing by sharing this inspiration? If so, who is it and how will I do it?

Mission Grace

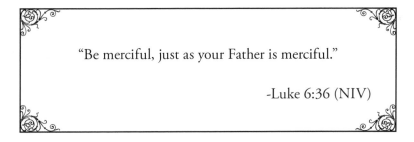

"Be merciful, just as your Father is merciful."

-Luke 6:36 (NIV)

Original Post—January 9, 2014

Mission Grace

The year 2013 was an awesome year, a gruesome year, a wonderful year, a chaotic year, a new beginning, a horrific ending, an enlightening experience, a torturous exploration and a most blessed year of the Lord. I know we suffered through way too many more examples of man's inhumanity to man this past year but there were many examples of compassion and kindness all around us as well. And on my personal ledger of positives and negatives in 2013, my graph shows more positive than negative happening for me (I needed that). I pray the same was true for you but even if it wasn't, my borrowed advice is to keep on living. We may be hurt (see *There's a Balm for That*) and slow it down or we may opt to just keep and pace and keep it moving rather than taking the time to reflect. Whatever the case, at the end of the day (or year), we are blessed to still be among the living; granted more time to get it as close to right as we can—granted grace.

One of the things on the positive side of my ledger is this season of football. I have watched some marvelous games this season, on all levels. I even attended two college bowl games (thank you gentlemen). I marvel at the physical skill and mental toughness of players on the college and professional level and I just appreciate efficient teams. While I believe all sports teach disciple and require attention to detail, adherence to instruction and to following leadership, football (and all the other team sports) requires and teaches more. One of the most prominent lessons is how to work on and within the framework of a team.

The dynamics of teamwork are fascinating and can be very delicate. There are team goals that override personal goals, desires and preferences. Everyone, particularly on the professional level, is capable and accomplished. Every teammate, in theory at least, is able to perform their given tasks. Having said that, being a good teammate sometimes means you have to let things go in order to preserve team-peace and preserve relationships. Sometimes it is better to just be encouraging or to be quiet rather than to risk fracturing a relationship; it is not necessary for teammates to point out blunders or errors. In the spiritual realm, it is called extending grace.

When I was working for the phone company, there was a cleaning lady I would talk to on the days I worked late. I tried hard not to be visibly surprised by anything she said to me about her life or her philosophies. One day she was telling me about a crime that had been committed in her neighborhood and she said "the crime is really getting bad and it's not just the blacks". I willed my face to remain blank and I simply said, "Yes ma'am, all races are committing crimes." In her mind, she was connecting with me and there was no need for me to wreck the connection; we were teammates with different functions. I would have gained nothing by arguing with her and being the little uppity black girl-engineer that worked in the cubicle off the north window. As Christians, we are called to be better!

Until I can give tangible gifts like Ellen DeGeneres, Dr. Patrick Angelo of Chicago or like the man who assisted Abigail Sailor with her educational endeavors, I can give grace. That is my goal for 2014; to extend more grace and to take advantage of every opportunity to teach my son to do the same. Building relationships can draw people into God's Kingdom. The extension of grace can win others to the side of Christ.

On the flip, damaging a relationship, by being right or being unyielding, serves no positive, eternal purpose. With regards to eternity, I want my personal ledger to show my graph with a lot more positive things than negative. Micah 6:8 is always the guide: "He has shown you, O mortal, what is good. And what does the Lord require of you? To act justly and to love mercy (grace) and to walk humbly with your God." Be about that life in 2014.

Regina

Probing Deeper:

What are my initial thoughts?

What did I learn or reinforce while reading this?

Can what I learned or reinforced help me with my daily life? If so, how?

Am I experiencing something right now that this particular inspiration can help me with?

Can I lighten the load someone else is experiencing by sharing this inspiration? If so, who is it and how will I do it?

Gifts of the Cross

"The mind governed by the flesh is death, but the mind governed by the Spirit is life and peace."

-Romans 8:6 (NIV)

Original Post—April 16,2014

Gifts of the Cross

I heard an actress, whom I'm not sure is a Christian, say that we need to listen to our inner voice in order to find confidence. Christian or not, she's right and the inner voice is that of the Holy Spirit. The Holy Spirit is one of the perpetual Gifts of the Cross. When Jesus told His disciples that He was going to leave them, He told them "I will ask the Father, and he will give you another Advocate to help you and be with you forever—the Spirit of Truth. The world cannot accept Him, because it neither sees Him nor knows Him. But you know Him, for he lives with you and will be in you (John 14:16-17)." He will be in us, helping us to transform more and more into the likeness of Christ; renewing our minds and turning our hearts into ceaseless fountains of love. We become the new creations that Paul talks about in 2 Corinthians 5:17.

Oh, the Gift of the Holy Spirit. We think we understand it but I'm really not convinced that we do. If we understood and could put it into practice—living the way the Spirit leads—we wouldn't struggle so much. Our lives would not be all roses and daisies but the peace we could have would surpass all understanding—in the midst of our storms. The struggles come because before we were saved, we developed habits and ways to survive and sometimes thrive without God. Good or bad we became familiar and comfortable with our methods. Back then, we were living according to our own wits; living according to the flesh. We no longer have to do that. We can turn responsibility for our existence over to the entire Trinity!

In addition to praying, God made provision for us when we have to respond in the moment; those times when we have an inkling or an urge that seems to come from nowhere. The issue comes because we have to choose to be led; we must choose to live by the Spirit and not according to the flesh. The conflict within us is real. Paul lays out the machinations manifested when following the flesh and then, the fruit produced when following the Spirit in Galatians 5:19-23. The fruit of the Spirit make us more like Christ and they aid us in our quest to draw others into the Kingdom of God. Following the flesh will lead to destruction and eternal damnation. It would seem that the choice(s) would be simple but it just isn't that easy.

Intellectually, we understand Galatians 5:19-23 and we do a decent job of following the Spirit. The thing is we tire of waiting. We are admonished to take our burdens to the Lord and leave them there but we don't. We pray for what we want and then refuse to follow the leading of the Spirit as we are being prepared for the blessings we have asked for. We start out following but then get frustrated when things don't happen in our time. So we figure we'll help God out (LOL). We are impatient or we don't recognize the preparation as helpful or essential so we fall back in line with our flesh; doing our own thing, trying to make things happen for ourselves. In Galatians 3:3, Paul asked the Galatians if they were foolish; "after beginning by means of the Spirit, are you now trying to finish by means of the flesh?" Are we foolish? Absolutely we are. But the occasions of our foolishness should be progressively less frequent, as children of God, siblings of Christ, carrying around the indwelling Holy Spirit as guide.

Kevin Ollie is such an inspirational man. After his playing days at the University of Connecticut (UConn) were over, he started paying dues in the CBA and the US Basketball league before making it into the NBA. He spent thirteen years as a vagabond with 11 teams. Ten-day and one-year contracts were the norm as God prepared him for his most recent achievement—for it is not over. Because of his previous trials and tribulations, Ollie was not shaken when he took over for Jim Calhoun and his job turned into something of a quagmire. From the NCAA sanctions to the initial six-month contract as UConn's leader to the communication skills he had to employ to keep some of his elite players from jumping ship, Ollie's commitment and conviction remained firm. The rocking of the waves and the fierceness of the storm has nothing to with who God is!

Ollie says his mission is to help develop young men; to help them access the Spirit within. Hello! God can do marvelous things for us if we acknowledge Him and allow Him to direct our paths (Proverbs 3:6). An acknowledging Kevin Ollie has guided his 2013-2014 team to the pinnacle of men's college basketball after just 18 months as the head coach. His achievement confounded the experts who were unfamiliar with God and His ways! Ollie says that he "will always bloom where he is planted, even if it is among weeds." Well he did because he definitely was. We should all have that understanding. Perhaps our trouble has to do with how we see our mission and define our success.

Charles Wesley wrote years ago, that our mission is defined as "A charge to keep I have, a God to glorify, a never-dying soul to save, and fit it for the sky. To serve the present age, my calling to fulfill; O may it all my powers engage to do my Master's will!" Paul said, in Galatians 2:20-21, that if we don't live according to the Spirit, Christ died for nothing (He most certainly did not!). Jesus said we could come to Him if we are weary and burdened down and He would give us soul-rest (Matthew 11:28-29). So perhaps we can effectively carry-out our mission (our charge) and achieve success when we cease to struggle and just follow the indwelling Spirit into the soul-rest that Jesus promised us. That, my dear brothers and sisters, sounds like a plan worthy of execution. Oh the perpetual Gifts of the Cross!

Regina

Probing Deeper:

What are my initial thoughts?

What did I learn or reinforce while reading this?

Can what I learned or reinforced help me with my daily life? If so, how?

Am I experiencing something right now that this particular inspiration can help me with?

Can I lighten the load someone else is experiencing by sharing this inspiration? If so, who is it and how will I do it?

Don't Get Weary

"Let us not become weary in doing good, for at the proper time we will reap a harvest if we do not give up."

-Galatians 6:9 (NIV)

Original Post—February 13, 2014

Don't Get Weary

Ray Nagin, Jesse Jackson, Jr., Bernard Kilpatrick, William J. Jefferson, Larry Langford, Kwame Kilpatrick, and, unfortunately, the list of politicians who started out doing great things, with great intentions and lost their way goes on. And it isn't just politicians. Preachers, teachers, mentors, parents, people; we start out with great intentions and with great ideas for positively changing our spheres of influence and existence and then we lose focus. Our eyes stop watching God. We get caught up, having allowed ourselves to get jaded and weary with the proverbial system. We can't do it! The price is too high.

I know there are things about life that cause us pain and anguish; things that absolutely bring us up short, leaving us speechless. But we can't act like we don't know who runs things. He gives us brand new mercies every morning so we can be about His business of showing grace (see Mission Grace) and showing restraint. The Bible puts it another way in Galatians 6:9, "Let us not become weary in doing good, for at the proper time we will reap a harvest if we do not give up."

When the Seahawks made it to the Super Bowl, I was ecstatic for Peter (Pete) Clay Carroll, because of Galatians 6:9 (and 2 Thessalonians 3:13). After Pete Carroll had been unceremoniously dismissed from the NFL by both the New York Jets and the New England Patriots, he had the opportunity to hone his craft and, more importantly his life's philosophy, at the University of Southern California and at his non-profit, A Better LA. His philosophy is based on the love of people; helping people release baggage, define goals and reach those goals. After nine years at USC and after making the program relevant and stout, Pete got the opportunity he thought he may never get, he could return to the NFL as a head coach with his now tested and proven philosophy intact and there would be room for Pete to start A Better Seattle.

Pete trains and empowers his assistant coaches to coach as if they are heads, not assistants. On Super Bowl Sunday 2014, every unit within the Seattle

Seahawks scored! Pete helps every member of his collective team clarify goals and maximize talent in order to reach those goals; he helps everybody become the best they can be, doing what they do with what they have. On Super Bowl Sunday, the youngest team in the NFL was focused and played as if they had been there before. And after just four years, with a previously down program, Pete made it to the NFL's grandest stage—and WON!! The swarming Legion of Boom shut down the league's most prolific offense. (The performance still makes me smile).

While Pete was in Los Angeles, building his success in order to build upon his success, God was busy. He was busy planting, coordinating, synchronizing and shifting things around in Seattle to accommodate Pete, Russell Wilson, Richard Sherman, Earl Thomas, Cliff Avril, MVP Malcolm Smith and Cam Chancellor, to name a few. Someone had been watching and Pete didn't get weary in doing good. It's amazing how God works!

A long, long, long time ago a guy named Joseph was sold into slavery by his brothers. His brothers were fed up with him because he was clearly his father's favorite and he seemed to place himself on a pedestal whenever he told his brothers and father about his dreams. He was purchased by Potiphar and was eventually entrusted with the entire management of Potiphar's affairs and household. Potiphar's wife desired him but Joseph wanted no parts of an affair. Scorned, the wife lied on Joseph and Potiphar threw him into prison.

Still, Potiphar trusted Joseph to run the operations at the jail and for Joseph's part, he never stopped doing good. He had to go through a cup-bearer and a baker in order to get to Pharaoh but he eventually did. The encounter landed him a prime-minister's role in Pharaoh's Egypt just in time to help his people—his family. Joseph kept gaining skills, developing his gifts and doing what was right and good before God, under all of his adverse circumstances and conditions. In the meantime, God was working it out so that Joseph would find favor with all he met and was in place and prepared at just the right time (Mordecai said it was "such a time as this" Esther 4:14); in Pharaoh's employ, with the power to effect change and impact lives.

Our current circumstances may be suffocating; we may pass through discouragement or become a regular visitor at the abode of despair but God runs this thing! The heat may be hot all around us and we may actually see the flames closing in but Isaiah 43:2 reminds us that the flames will not consume us. That verse of scripture also tells us that we will not drown, even if we see the water mounting, in the form of bills or notices or whatever—we will not drown. If we will just wait on His will and His timing, we can look forward to mounting up on wings as eagles but if not that, we can run and not get weary or if not that, we can walk and not faint (Isaiah 40:31). The Lord has preserving power! So "Walk together children. Don't you get weary. There's a great camp meeting in the promised land!" (Walk together Children, composer John Rosamond Johnson, 1915).

Regina

Probing Deeper:

What are my initial thoughts?

What did I learn or reinforce while reading this?

Can what I learned or reinforced help me with my daily life? If so, how?

Am I experiencing something right now that this particular inspiration can help me with?

Can I lighten the load someone else is experiencing by sharing this inspiration? If so, who is it and how will I do it?

Acknowledgments

I want to extend a general thank you to anyone who ever impacted my life and had a hand in me becoming the woman I am. Having said that, I want to thank my friends and loved ones, most of whom were readers of the initial blogs. I especially want to thank every one of you who took the time to give me feedback and encouragement regarding them. The list is voluminous so I'll refrain from naming names and offending somebody whose name was inadvertently omitted. Instead, just let me say that I sincerely appreciate and am indebted to all of you for your support. I wasn't sure where the blogs were going but my cousin suggested I "do something" with them (thanks Janiece) and here we are.

I want to thank my pastor, Rev. Dr. E. W. Lee, and the Shiloh Baptist Church family, especially Mrs. Cooper and all the ladies of the Wisdom of Ages Ministry group. You ladies always encourage and support me and I really enjoy the times you let me come in to share a Word with you. I get to go deeper every time I get before God's people. Thank you to everybody who has given me the opportunity to come before your group or congregation to speak a Word from God. Thank you to my chapter (Xi Beta Omega) sorority sisters of Alpha Kappa Alpha for allowing me to serve you as Chaplain and for the kind embracing of me in the role.

I want to thank the writers of Christian fiction (and Walter Mosely). There are some book series that really inspired me and made me realize that I could get to the heart of the issues that face people every day and I could help without the rigidity that comes from some Christian forums. The authors of the books relate freedom in using God's Word to help their characters and tell their stories of redemption.

And finally, I want to thank my family. My dad has gone on to glory but his influence is still a major part of who I am and how I live my life and do my part in raising Braelon. My mom, Artelia Reese, doesn't always get me but she always supports whatever I do and loves me in spite of her misgivings about something I'm doing or not doing. Thank you mama.

To my husband, Al, I say thank you. We've known each other a very long time and have been married for what seems like longer (laugh with me) so we sometimes take each other for granted. Let me tell you that I did not take the time you spent reading and re-reading for granted. I am very grateful for your love, your time, your prayers and your presence. To our son, Braelon, my illustrator, thank you for being you. Your joy and laughter are infectious. I am mightily blessed and am most assuredly highly favored to have you in my life. I do my best to honor God in raising you every day. Thank you for being you and inspiring me to be better. Thank you to My brother, Renford Reese, Ph.D., the other writing offspring. I used to maintain that I was the real writer in the family, after daddy, but you're the man.

And to my extended family, by blood and according to the heart (Barges, Nettles, Floyds, Calhouns, Sylvesters, Gonsal, Whites to name a *few*), thank you for all you have meant to me and my immediate family. As George Wallace often says, "I love you and there is absolutely nothing you can do about it."

Regina

Introduction to a future work

I was doing my mandatory internship with a Christian Counseling practice a few towns over from my house and this day was the day I was to go through another counseling session—as the client. The practice was run by a husband and wife team and I had already gone through my session, as client, with the husband. My background made me most comfortable with him. In addition, his objective was not to go deep into my psyche. His job was to show me how to ask questions. I had even been invited to sit with him during a couple of his sessions, with the client's approval of course. I really enjoyed watching him work and I enjoyed my session with him as client. I thought it was instructive and very beneficial.

His wife's objectives were apparently different. She wanted to pry and poke and—in my opinion—get me to cry so she would know that she had gotten to the core of my emotions. I was six months pregnant, so she was probably sure she could get to it quickly. At that moment, I was irritable. I was sitting directly across from her. We were separated by just a few feet of air. She really wanted my hormones to see her. It was close to lunchtime and I'm always irritable if I'm sleepy or hungry. I was hungry and wanting her to get this over with. She asked the standard questions and then she asked about my pregnancy. I told her it had been going well up until I put salt on a green apple. The swelling had come but I was not sick as a result. Ha ha ha, we laughed and I thought I was on my way to lunch. Not so fast sister!

Next were questions about other pregnancies. I paused and started looking around the room, wondering who had told her. Lord! I needed to finish this internship for my this degree, so I felt that my options for protest were few. Geez, I wanted direction on being the counselor and I was not sure how this was helping. This whole experience was not turning out the way I had expected. Oh well, it had to be endured and I knew my mood would have little bearing on her agenda so I decided to suck it up and do what I had to do to get through this. I silently prayed for help and thought of the food on the other side of the encounter for motivation. And so she had asked about other pregnancies.

I told her I had been pregnant three times before and each had resulted in miscarriages for different reasons. I rushed on to assure her that I was fine; that only the third one had knocked me a little off-balance. She gave me a hard stare but didn't reach to embrace me. I had convinced her and we were moving on. I can really be naïve sometimes. She paused for about 30 seconds and then it was clear that she didn't believe that I was fine. She dug deeper. At what stage of the pregnancies had the problems been identified? Was it a family matter or did we have to deal with questions from others? What did I do after each one; take a few days off, get depressed, jump over the hump and continue as usual? Had I given the children names and had I said goodbye with a formal ceremony for each of them? WHAT?!!

I looked at her pretty hard then and determined that I had better come up with something because she needed to help me; she needed to help me cope with the losses that had not crippled or depressed me. Think girl, is what I was telling myself. We had chosen names for the first and second presences but didn't choose another name until this one that I was carrying. So, I gave her the names I had, having pulled the third name from my maternal grandfather. Then I had to answer the part about the ceremonies. I was reaching the outer limits of my politeness, but I took a deep breath and said no, I had not had three ceremonies because I was okay with God's will. She smiled politely and nodded in a sort of knowing manner at me and then she told me to close my eyes while she prayed. I was really starting to feel uncomfortable but I sucked in some more air and did as I was told.

I listened intently to her prayer, hoping that I could get some indication as to what I was supposed to do next. When she finished praying, she asked that I keep my eyes closed and tell her what I saw. What?!! I swallowed hard and followed her prayer lead. I told her I saw Jesus. She didn't sound surprised. She moved right on to ask what I was doing in His presence. I told her I was sitting in His lap; I was being rocked in the arms of Jesus!

It looked like I had hit the proverbial pay-dirt. I opened my eyes and saw the look on her face. She looked so satisfied with herself. And I declare that's what I really saw. I'm just not sure if I saw it before she asked or if I had painted the frame in my mind as I was saying it. It was surreal, but I wasn't so happy about it. I was wiping away tears now and I was ticked off because she had made me do this even though I was fine. Now I had to revisit my feelings and the timing was not of my choosing.

I grew up a sort of idealistic realist. I am the eldest of two; the flawed evolution of the people who are my flawed but perfect parents (for me). My path and journey have been heavily influenced, and largely navigated, by two people borne of the Deep South but with very different seats on the bus that was their (largely) common experiences. Survival was often the objective and rule of the day for my genius dad, while my mother got the nurturing and support that pushed her to college at age 16. God was a distant Deity to both of them; living and loving but distant. Yet they maintained their belief in Him, albeit as a sort of fallback—a safety net in times of trouble. They, particularly my daddy, had scars and lingering wounds from childhood. They had come of age within environments that pushed and celebrated self-reliance. Consequently, I grew up with a slightly warped view of who God truly is and how He intends for us to respond to Him every day, every hour and every minute of the day. So now I sat, having to reflect on a lot of things because this woman just wouldn't leave well-enough alone.

A few comments about current volume of writings

<u>Regarding Gifts of the Cross</u>

- Regina, this particular blog "great", if made available to all, I think, could reach out to touch everyone that is in a needy position to be directed by a higher power; "could really touch a few empty souls" and capture the fleeting spirits of souls that are borderline and confused about life and living. Stay the course because your journey has just begun!
- Wow, Regina another great blog, one that I really needed to hear. I am not really a sports person but I always did enjoy the final four and I was rooting for coach Ollie and UConn. He inspired me this morning as I was listening to him do an interview on the radio.

<u>Regarding Don't Get Weary</u>

- Regina, you wrote some powerful, encouraging words that will make anyone stand firm on God's promises when you're going through a fierce storm. Thank you, and may God continue to empower you in His word.
- Thank you very much for sharing this message! I must admit there have been many times in which I have felt discouraged and wondered why I am at a certain station in my life, career, etc. Your message—along with God's word has definitely put things in perspective for me. It was right on time!

<u>Regarding Mission Grace</u>

- Regina, AWESOME!!! God has "Blessed" you with a special gift of communicating, inspiring and challenging each of us in our Christian Walk. I too am a Sports Enthusiast and will be praying for my Football Team. :) You have reminded us that every situation is not a battle nor does it have to be addressed, sometimes, it is just a teaching moment and God is saying, Listen and Learn.

- Hello Regina, you are always an inspiration to me. I had plans for the year 2014 but you have added to make it better for me. You are a very special person and this is a gift God has Blessed you with. Please continue to share.

Regarding The Favor of God

- It is true that sometimes you have to take 2 steps backwards in order to move forward. Thank you for bringing that back to my attention.
- Awesome words to inspire us to "stay in His presence". It is not always easy . . . ao many distractions. Yet, in His presence, we are overcomers! Thanks for the reminder—such an uplifting piece! I am encouraged!

About the Author

Regina R. Tate is a Christian Counselor. She has always loved to write but was pushed away from her dream of being a sports writer long ago. Now, she feels like she has come back around to her dream, just not in the way she envisioned it. She sees the awesomeness of God in that she is realizing her original dream while at the same time exercising her other passion – helping those who hurt, according to the Word of God.

Regina is a past engineer with a phone company and a paper company. She has worked for a car manufacturer and as an assistant to her church pastor. She holds a Bachelor of Science degree in Mechanical Engineering, a Master's degree in Human Resource Development and a Master of Arts degree in Christian Counseling. She has had audiences with business leaders, government officials, politicians, academicians and gatherings of the Lord's people. She does not consider herself an expert on the Word of God, nor is she an expert in all things sports. She does believe that the totality of her journey thus far has given her a unique way to help those who hurt. She and her husband of twenty years, Al Tate, have one son, Braelon, and they reside in McDonough, Georgia.